Fill

In

The

Blanks

To Learning

Android 4

(Ice Cream Sandwich)

By Reginald T. Prior

Visit http://www.rcsbooks.com or E-Mail me at reginaldprior@rcsbooks.com

Printed in the United States of America

First Printing: February 2012

ISBN - 978-1469952970

EAN - 1469952971

Trademarks And Copyrights

Trademarked and or copyrighted names appear throughout this book. Rather than list and name the entities, names or companies that own the trademark and or copyright or insert a trademark or copyright symbol for with every mention of the trademarked and or copyrighted name, The publisher and the author states that it is using the names for editorial purposes only and to benefit the trademark and or copyright owner, with no intentions of infringing on the trademark and or copyrights.

Warning and Disclaimer

Every effort has been made to make this book as complete and accurate as possible. No warranties are implied. The information provided is on a "as is" basis. The author and the publisher have no liability or responsibility to any individuals or entities with any respect to any loss or damages from the information provided in this book.

Preface

There are many books on the market that teach people how to use technology. But as I look through many of these books, I have found that they teach some of the basics, but miss a lot of critical things about how to fully utilize technology.

My aim of this book is to fill in these gaps that most books don't cover or spend sufficient time covering in common sense and in a way that is easily understood by everyone. As a computer technician for 12 years, I've come across many people that understand some things about technology, but want to have a better understanding about how it works and how to fully utilize them in their everyday lives.

In this book, I will be covering Google's Android 4.0 (Ice Cream Sandwich) Operating System. Android 4.0 is the first version of Android that will be created for both cellular phones and tablet computers. In previous versions of Android, either it was created for smartphones (In the case of Android version 1 & 2) or for tablets (In the case of Android 3).

Because of this, the Android user experience greatly varied from version to version. The next few pictures show the home screens from version 1.0 to the current version 4.0:

Android 1.0 (Cupcake, Donut, Eclair) Android 2.0 (Froyo & Gingerbread)

Android 3.0 (Honeycomb)

Android 4.0 (Ice Cream Sandwich)

Apple's IOS products have a slight but significant advantage over Google's Android products by having a consistent look and feel from one product to another. That in turn shortens the learning curve for end consumer to learn how to use that product. Android 4 aims to end that advantage.

You as the reader are the most important critics of this book. I value all of your feedback and suggestions that you may have for future books and other things that I can do to make these books better. You can e-mail me at reginaldprior@rcsbooks.com and please include the book title, as well as your name and e-mail address. I will review your comments and suggestions and will keep these things in mind when I write future texts. Thank you in advance,

Reginald T. Prior

Acknowledgements

This book that you are reading right now takes a lot of time and sacrifice to put together. I would first and foremost thank God for giving me at the age of six the love of working on technology that still is as strong today as it was back then. I would like to thank my wife, Sharifa for being a trooper when I was spending many hours on my laptop putting this book together and also for being there to help me read my drafts to make sure that it would be understood.

Also I would like to thank my family and many friends that helped and supported me throughout the years on many other projects and being there for me in good times and bad. I hope that you all enjoy this book as much as I had putting it together.

Hello Everyone,

I would like to thank you in advance for purchasing "Fill In The Blanks To Understanding Android 4.0" I aim to make the Google Android operating system easy to learn while showing you the many features that Google has implemented to make Android the choice of many computer manufacturers for use with Cell Phones & Tablet Computers.

Table Of Contents:

Chapter One: Touch Screen Computers Terminology Dictionary

Touch Screen Device Terminology Dictionary ----------------------------11
How To Turn Your Android Device On And Off ------------------------- 17

Chapter Two: Getting To Know Android 4.0

Navigating The Main Android Screen --------------------------------------24
What Does All Of These Buttons Do? --------------------------------------29
Making Phone Calls On Your Device (Smartphone Option) ----------32
Answering or Denying Calls (Smartphone Option) ----------------------34
How To Send Texts (Smartphone Option) ---------------------------------35
How To Tell What Version Of Android You Have ----------------------40
How To Add/Remove App Icons From Home Screens ----------------42
How To Create Folders To Organize App Icons -------------------------44
Setting Options Through The Settings Menu ---------------------------46
Changing The Notification & Ringtone ---------------------------------- 49
How To Connect Your Device To Wi-Fi Hotspots ----------------------51
Setting Up Bluetooth Devices --53
Enabling The New Data Usage Monitoring Feature -------------------56
Using The New Android Beam Feature --------------------------------------61
Adding Contacts & Phone Numbers --63
Deleting Contacts ---67
How To Get Onto The Internet --69
Using Tabs To Navigate Multiple Websites --------------------------------74
How To Bookmark Websites --77
How To Setup And Use E-Mail ---81
Sending Email From Your Device --88
Deleting Email From Your Device ---93

Using The Camera To Take Pictures And Video --------------------------95

How To Download & View Pictures On Your Device --------------------98

Using The Gallery To Delete Pictures & Video--------------------------108

How To Download Music To Your Device --------------------------------110

Using The Music App To View And Play Your Music --------------------116

Chapter Three: Using The Android Market To Add Functionality To Your Android Device

Getting To & Looking Through The Android Market ------------------124

Installing Apps On Your Device -- --125

Uninstalling Apps That You Don't Use -----------------------------------131

Chapter Four: Mobile Device Security

The Three Things You Can Do To Protect Your Data And Your Android Device From Cyber Thieves And Other Threats--------------------------136

Using The New Face Scan Unlock Feature ----------------------------- 145

Other Cool Things To Do With Your Android Device -----------------157

Chapter One:

Touch Screen Terminology Dictionary

Chapter One: Technology Terminology Dictionary

Before we go into learning how to operate Android or any other operating system, I believe that before you can have knowledge about anything, you have to build your knowledge like a builder builds a house. First you have to lay a solid foundation down before we can start building floors and rooms within the house. Understanding the terminology and what it means is like laying the foundation on the house.

This chapter translates what we geeks talk about when we are talking about Android-based devices. Decode the foreign language so to speak. This is not a full list of tech terminology, but this is a list of the most common terminology used for talking about most touch screen devices. So with no further delays, let's get started laying the foundation to being confident to use your Android Device.

Note - When you go to purchase an Android-based device, you would need to have a Gmail or a Google account already setup. First go to http://www.gmail.com to sign up for a FREE account. You need to do this because all of your Android devices need to link with a Google account to download apps, perform automatic backups of your contacts and other information, and for your Android device to take advantage of all of Google's other services.

Tablet Computers–

Tablet Computers are a category of mobile device (Usually with screen sizes 7 inches and larger) that provides advanced capabilities beyond a typical laptop or other mobile device. Tablets will have a touchscreen and run complete operating system software that provides a standardized look and feel.

QWERTY –

The term that commonly describes today's standard keyboard layout on English-language computers.

Accelerometer-

Sensors inside the device that measures tilt and motion. A device with an accelerometer knows what angle it is being held at. It can also measure movements such as rotation, and motion gestures such as swinging, shaking, and flicking.

One common use is to detect whether the Device is upright or sideways and automatically rotate the graphics on the screen accordingly. Another common use is controlling games and other applications (such as music player) by moving or shaking the Device.

Left And Right Swipe –

The action of touching the screen of the device and sliding your finger to the left for a Left Swipe, or to the right for a Right Swipe. Commonly used to navigate between screens on your Device.

The next pictures show examples of both left and right swiping.

Left Swiping

Right Swiping

14

Up And Down Swipe –

The action of touching the device and sliding your finger up for an Up Swipe, or down for a Down Swipe. Commonly used to navigate, show more options on a menu, or to navigate more of the webpage in your browser.

Single/Double Tap –

The action of touching the device and quickly release once for single tap, twice for double tap. Commonly used to select or activate something. (Think of this as single or double clicking the mouse button on your computer)

Geo-Tagging-

Geo-tagging is associating a geographic location with an item such as a photo. Some Devices with both a camera and GPS can record the precise location a photo was taken and automatically embed that location information into the photo file.

GPS –

GPS (Global Positioning System) is a global satellite-based system for determining precise location on Earth. In a Device, this will allow operators to immediately receive your location when you call the emergency number (911 or 112).

Multi-Touch –

The ability for a touch surface to respond to multiple finger touches at the same time. For example, a common use for multi-touch is pinch-to-zoom, where you can place two fingers on a screen image (like photo, web page, or map) and spread your fingers to zoom in, or pinch your fingers together to zoom out.

3G-

3G Stands for 3rd-generation. Analog cellular phones with just voice capability are considered first generation. Cellular Phones with texting capabilities marked the second generation (2G). 3G is loosely defined, but generally includes high data speeds, streaming video and always-on data access, and greater voice capacity.

4G –

A somewhat vague term used to describe wireless mobile radio technologies that offer up to 10 times faster data rates than current 3G (third generation) technologies.

The Cloud or Cloud Computing

Cloud computing refers to applications and services offered over the Internet. These services are offered from data centers all over the world, which collectively are referred to as the "cloud." This metaphor represents the intangible, yet universal nature of the Internet.

Examples of cloud computing include online backup services, App Stores such as Google's Android Market, Apple's App Store or Amazon's App Store. It also includes personal data services such as Apple's Mobile Me. Cloud computing also includes online applications such as Facebook.

Smartphone –

Smart phones are a category of mobile device that provides advanced capabilities beyond a typical mobile phone. Smartphone's run complete operating system software that provides a standardized look and feel

Turning On And Off Your Android Device

The first thing that has to be done before we can start working with an Android device is to have your device turned on. Every Android device is made differently and manufacturers place the power button in many different places. But the one thing you need to keep in mind is that the power button has an icon that looks like the picture below:

To turn your device on, find the button that has the icon that looks like the picture shown above and press and hold down that button. After about 5 seconds, your Android device should turn on and then you can let go of that button.

To turn your Android device off, you will press and hold down the same button, and a menu choice will come up looking like the next picture:

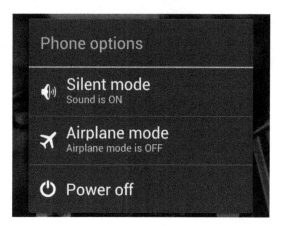

At this prompt, single tap the "Power off" option. After single tapping that option, another prompt will come up looking like the next picture:

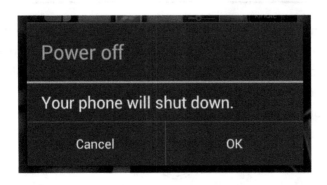

Now, single tap the "OK" button. After you single tapped the "OK" button, the device will then turn off.

Putting Your Android Device Into Sleep Mode

You can put Android device to sleep mode while it is ON anytime. Just **press and release the power button** to activate sleep mode on your Android device. To turn it back on, just press and release the power button again to go back to the unlock screen where you would single tap on the lock icon and hold your finger on the screen. The screen should look similar to the next picture:

Then swipe your finger to the right to the unlocked lock icon to unlock your phone. The camera icon to the left is the face activated unlock mode that is new to Android 4, which we will discuss later in this book.

Chapter Two:

Getting To Know Your Android 4 Device

Over the years, trends in technology have changed. One trend was the shift from using desktop computers to notebook computers. This change happened because people had started to be more mobile and needed to use a computer on the go. So notebook computers became more popular than a desktop.

But for the past year or so, technology is currently in process of another trend happening. Mobile devices are suddenly able to do as much or more than a notebook computer, but in a smaller package. So more people are now swapping their notebooks for these powerful mobile devices.

This trend is going to continue to explode due to the fact that Device computers and cellular phones can do all of the same things as a notebook like sending and receiving email, playing games, surfing the Internet, and installing and running other applications.

After you have pushed the power button on your Android device and turned it on, your device will do a quick hardware check. After that check has completed, a "Master Program" will start up called the operating system. That process is called booting up.

The booting up process is the act of the device setting up everything it needs to operate. Once Android has fully booted up, it will go right to the main screen where you would swipe right on the lock icon to the unlock icon to start using your Device. The picture below shows what that screen looks like.

Navigating The Main Android Screen (For Smartphones)

After you have swiped the lock icon to the unlock icon to unlock your Android Device, you will be presented with the main screen as shown in the next picture.

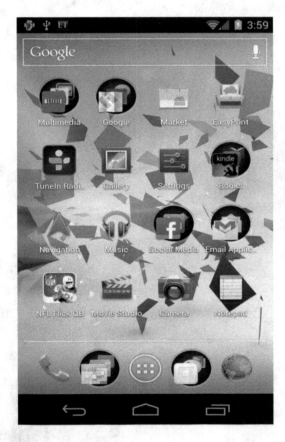

In the following sections, we will go over in detail about everything you see on the main screen of an Android Ice Cream Sandwich device. The next picture shows the most important things to keep in mind when you look at the main screen on your Android device:

24

- The Application or Launch Icon is where you would single tap to view all of the apps currently on your Android device.

- The Notification or Status Bar shows information including the time, battery status, signal strength and other information. The next picture shows all of the Notification Icons that also will show up here also.

M	New Gmail message		3 more notifications not displayed
	New text or multimedia message		Call in progress
!	Problem with text or multimedia message delivery		Call in progress using Bluetooth head-set
talk	New Google Talk™ message		Missed call
OO	New voicemail		Call on hold
1	Upcoming event		Call forwarding is on
	Data is syncing	1	Uploading data
⚠	Problem with sign-in or sync		Downloading data
	microSD card is full		Download finished
?	An open Wi-Fi network is available		Connected to VPN
	Phone is connected via USB cable		Disconnected from VPN
►	Song is playing		

- The Application Icon allows you single tap an icon to start a specific Application. Think about this as a shortcut on your Windows or Macintosh computer.

Note – You are not limited to using the icons that the Device comes with by default. You can add or remove icons from any one of your home screens. This will be explained more in detail later in this chapter.

New in Android 4 is the dock area (Smartphones Only) where you can place application icons & folders for easy and quick access. This will be explained more in detail later in this chapter.

Navigating The Main Android Screen (For Tablets)

If you have an Android 4 tablet, you will be presented with the main screen as shown in the next picture:

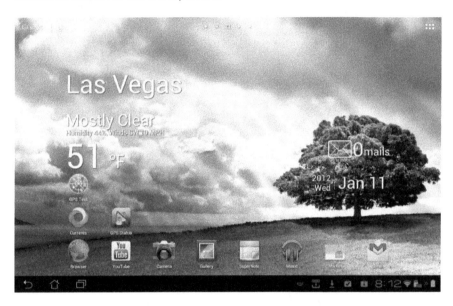

In the following sections, we will go over in detail about everything you see on the main screen of an Android Ice Cream Sandwich tablet. The next picture shows the most important things to keep in mind when you look at the main screen on your Android device:

- The Application or Launch Icon is where you would single tap to view all of the apps currently on your Android device.

- The Application Icon allows you single tap an icon to start a specific Application. Think about this as a shortcut on your Windows or Macintosh computer.

- The Notification or Status Bar shows information including the time, battery status, signal strength and other information. The next picture shows all of the Notification Icons that also will show up here also.

M	New Gmail message		3 more notifications not displayed
	New text or multimedia message		Call in progress
!	Problem with text or multimedia message delivery		Call in progress using Bluetooth head-set
talk	New Google Talk™ message		Missed call
oo	New voicemail		Call on hold
1	Upcoming event		Call forwarding is on
	Data is syncing	1	Uploading data
⚠	Problem with sign-in or sync		Downloading data
	microSD card is full		Download finished
	An open Wi-Fi network is available		Connected to VPN
	Phone is connected via USB cable		Disconnected from VPN
▶	Song is playing		

Note – You are not limited to using the icons that the Device comes with by default. You can add or remove icons from any one of your home screens. This will be explained more in detail later in this chapter.

What Does All Of These Buttons Do?

Before we go into actually using your Android Device computer, first we have to go over the function buttons and what explain they are used for, because you will use them a lot. These buttons are located on the bottom left of the Device screen. These are pictures are from a Galaxy Nexus smartphone, but all Android devices have similar buttons.

- This is the back button on your Android Device. This button is used for multiple functions. One function of this button is to go back to a previous screen within the Device or a previous webpage when surfing the Internet.

- This is the home button on your Android Device. This button is used to take you back to the main screen from anywhere.

- This is the menu key. This is one of the most important functionality keys on the Android Device. This key is most commonly used to provide additional options for your Device or within an application. Think of this button as your "File" menu within any Windows program. This icon will show up only when there are additional options for that particular application.

- This is the recent apps button. When you press this button, a list of all of the apps you have been in recently will come up on the screen where you can swipe up or down and single tap the app to go into it (Similar to Windows 7 Aero). Your screen will look similar to the next picture:

Note – Sometimes when you are in an app or on some menus, the function buttons will hide and look similar to the next picture:

single tap anywhere on this section to show the navigation buttons again.

30

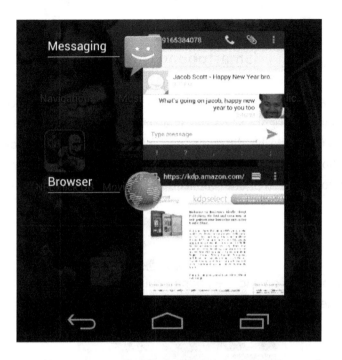

Note – A new feature in Ice Cream Sandwich is the option to force close applications to conserve your devices internal memory. Swipe up or down in this menu, then swipe right on the application you are not using to close the app.

- This is your web search button. It is located at the top part of the home screen. Single tap the Google logo and type in the dialog box to do a web search on Google.

Quick Tip - If you single tap the microphone icon, A window will pop up telling you to "Speak now." Do so, and Google will automagically search for whatever you said

Making A Call On Your Device
(Smartphone Option Only)

The one main thing that you want to do on your Android Device is to make phone calls right? Since this is a smartphone, buttons and other functions are a little bit different than on a regular cellular phone. To make a phone call on Android, Single tap the launch icon and swipe up or down to find the phone application. The icon looks like the next picture:

Single tap on the icon and the phone application will then come up and look like the next picture:

Use the touchscreen to dial the number you wish to call. If you mistype in a number, use the delete icon to delete and correct the number then single tap the call button when you have the number correct which looks like the next picture:

Then your phone will dial the number you have just entered into the phone and the screen will look like the next picture:

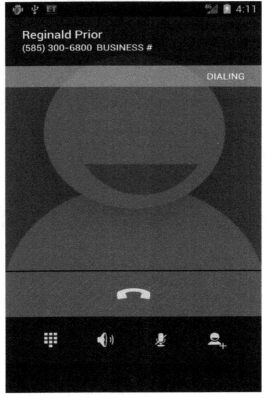

As you notice when you are in a call, there are four icons at the bottom of this screen. We are to explain what each one of those icons mean at this time.

- This icon displays the keypad during calls

 - This icon allows you to add more people to the call during calls (Conference Calling Feature)

 - This icon mutes and unmutes your microphone during calls

 - This icon turns on and off the speakerphone option during calls

To end the current call, single tap the red end call button icon which looks like this ▬, and the phone will end the current call.

Answering/Denying A Call On Your Phone (Smartphones Only)

You are doing something and your phone suddenly rings. And you find that answering a phone call on your Android device is a little different from a regular cellular phone. When a phone call comes in, the screen of your Android phone will look similar to the next picture

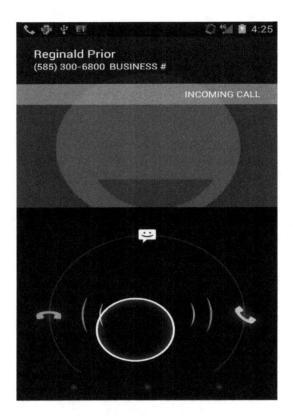

To answer the call, you would touch the center circle and swipe right the green answer icon to answer the phone. To send the caller to voicemail, swipe left the red deny call icon.

How To Send A Text To Someone (Smartphone Option Only)

Another thing you can do with your Android device is to send a text to another person's cell phone. To do that, single tap the launch icon from the main screen (You would get to the main screen by pressing the home key on your phone. It look like this⌂) single tap the launch icon and swipe left or right to find the messaging application. Find the messaging icon which looks like the next picture,

And single tap on it. Then the messaging app will come up looking like the next picture:

Next single tap the "New Message" icon which looks like this  to pull up the new message window as shown in the next picture:

Single tap the "To" box and the touch keyboard will come up on the screen where you would type in the cellular phone number of the person you want to send the text to (Area Code first).

Note – You would have to single tap on the "?123" key to display the numbers keypad where you can type numbers in the "To" textbox.

If you have some cellular contacts already in your address book, then they should show up where you can swipe up or down and single tap on a specific person as shown in the next picture:

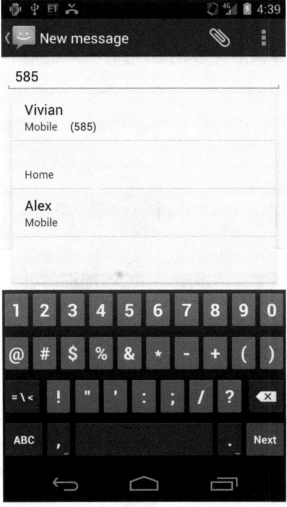

Once you have entered the phone number of the person you want to send this text to, single tap the "Type To Compose" text box and type

your message. When you are done, single tap the "Send" button .
Your screen should look like the next picture:

When the other person sees the text, they would respond back and their texts will appear in this same window with the time that they had sent it. that is how you would send a text to someone on your Android 4 Device.

What Version Of Android Do I Have?

At the time of the writing of this book, there are two versions of Android Ice Cream Sandwich operating system. There is version 4.0.1 and version 4.0.2. Both versions are covered in this book.

You might be asking yourself, how do I know what version of Android my particular device has? On the main screen (You would get to the main screen by pressing the "Home" key on your Device. It would look like this ⌂), then single tap the launch icon which is located at the center bottom part of the screen and looks like this ⊞ and the app screen will come up like the next picture:

Swipe left or right until you see the "Settings" icon which would look like the following picture below:

Single tap this icon and the settings screen should look like the next picture:

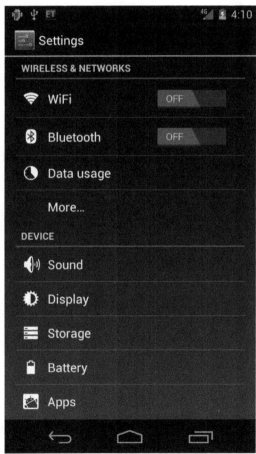

Swipe up and single tap the "About Phone" or the "About Tablet" option. Look at the Android Version line in this menu. Whatever your device displays in this line is the version of Android your device presently is running. After you have checked the version of Android, Press the home key to go back to the main screen.

To Remove an Application Icon From Your Home Screen:

1. Touch and hold the application icon that you wish to remove from the home screen. The Device will vibrate and you should notice a trash can with the words "Remove" located at the top section of the screen as shown in the next picture:

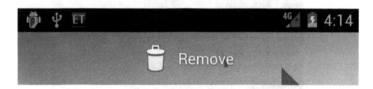

2. Drag the icon with your finger to the trash can icon and let go of the icon. The icon is now removed from your home screen.

To Add an Application Icon To Your Home Screen:

1. Single tap the launch icon. Swipe left or right to find the application you want to put on your home screen.

2. Touch and hold the desired application you want on your home screen. The device will vibrate and a window showing all five of your home screens will appear as shown in the next picture:

Drag the icon left or right to the specific home screen you desire to put this shortcut and let go of the icon to add the application to that particular home screen.

Note – You can have multiple home screens on an Android device. Most devices allow you to have at least 5 home screens where you can add application icons, folders or Widgets to show different kinds of information.

To go to another home screen, just left or right swipe on the home screen and your Device will transition to the next home screen. To get back to the main home screen, just press the home key on your Device.

To Create Folders On Any Home Screen To Categorize Apps:

Quickly finding our favorite Apps on the Android Home Screens can sometimes be difficult. Sometimes you simply run out of room for all of your Apps! Sifting through all of your Apps in the launch menu isn't fun either. The best way to organize your Android Home Screens is to create Folders to store apps. You can create folders to organize your apps into different categories like Games, Music, Productivity, Social Networks, etc. The nice thing about folders is that they allow you to group apps in a neat and organized way.

To quickly create a folder on your home screen, just drag one icon on top of another one. When you do that, a circle forms around both icons as shown in the next picture:

Let go of the icon to create the folder. It will be an unnamed folder. To create a name for the new folder, just single tap on it and it will look like the next picture:

Single tap on the words "Unnamed Folder", and the field will then clear and the touch keyboard will come up. Type a suitable name for this folder, then single tap anywhere on the home screen to assign that name to this folder. To remove the folder, just single tap on the folder icon and hold it down until the trash can icon with the words "Remove" appear at the top of the screen. Drag the folder icon to it and let go to delete the folder from the home screen.

<u>Setting Options Through The Settings Menu</u>

There are times you need to change the way your Android device operates. You would to go to the settings menu to accomplish this. The settings menu at first glance can be very intimidating because there are so many options. But we only need to be concerned with a couple of selections at this time.

To get to the settings menu, on the main screen (You would get to the main screen by pressing the "Home" key on your Device. It would look like this ⬜), Then single tap the launch icon which is located at the bottom center part of the screen and looks like this and the app screen will come up like the next picture:

Swipe left or right until you see the "Settings" icon which would look like the following picture below:

Single tap this icon and the settings screen should look like the next picture:

Like I had mentioned earlier in this section, the settings menu can be intimidating, but we need to only at this time be concerned with only a few options here:

1. Wireless & Network Settings – This is the section where you would put your device into "Airplane Mode", configure Bluetooth devices such as hands free earpieces or connect to local Wi-Fi hotspots.

2. Sound Settings – This is the section where you can assign different ringtones or sounds for events that happen on your device.

We are about to go into detail of the options in the Sound menu. Single tap that menu selection to go into that menu. Your screen should look like the next picture:

In this menu, a lot of the menu choices are self-explanatory. To change the notification sound for your device, single tap the "Default Notification" option and a dialog box will come up, showing all of the notification ringtones that are available on your device. It will look like the next picture:

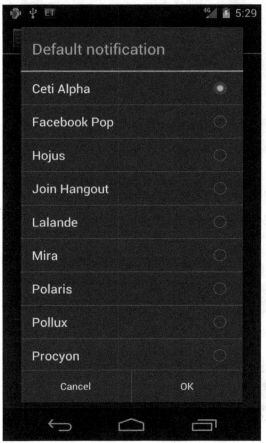

Swipe up or down through selection of tones. Select a tone by single tapping on it and a sample sound will play. If you like it, single tap the "OK" button and that notification ringtone will be set on your device, or single tap the cancel button and nothing would be changed.

To change the ringtone for your device, single tap the "Phone Ringtone" option and a dialog box will come up, showing all of the ringtones that are available on your device. It will look like the next picture:

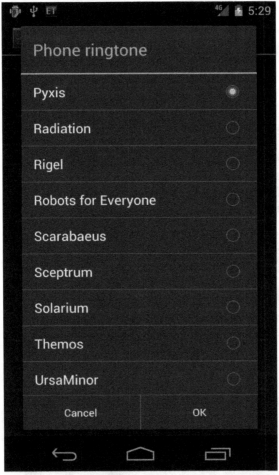

Swipe up or down through selection of ringtones. Select a ringtone by single tapping on it and a sample sound will play. If you like it, single tap the "OK" button and that ringtone will be set on your device, or single tap the cancel button and nothing would be changed. To go back to the settings menu, single tap the back button.

The next set of options that we will now cover is the "Wireless & Network Settings" section.

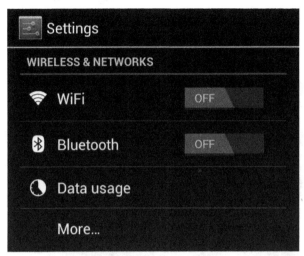

There are many options on this menu and the menu choices and the phrases that are used may be new to you, so I am going to explain what they mean and why you should know about them.

Wi-Fi Mode – Your device is capable of connecting to Wi-Fi hot spots as well as the Internet connection provided by your cell phone carrier. The advantage of this is that you can enjoy the same high speed wireless lines that you would on your laptop.

Also when you are downloading updates to your Device (Which we would go over In the Android Market chapter) or music files from Amazon, the downloads would be faster than it would be strictly on your wireless carrier's Internet connection. Also if don't have a unlimited data plan (Wireless carriers pretty much eliminated this practice), then you can enjoy using your Device for surfing the Internet without fear of overage charges.

To switch your device onto WI-FI mode, single tap the "off" option on the Wi-Fi line to enable WI-FI mode. Then single tap the "Wi-Fi Mode" menu choice, and the Wi-Fi menu show up like the next picture:

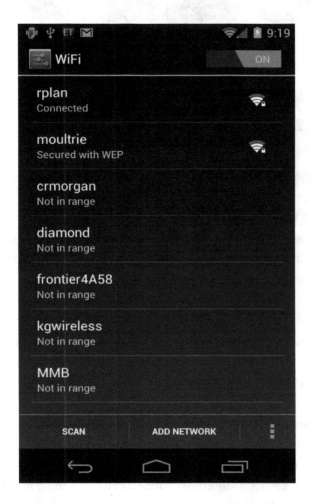

In this menu, your device will scan for the nearest Wi-Fi access points and list them in this menu.

To connect to a particular access point, then single tap on that access point label, and if it requires a password, the Device will prompt for a password as shown in the next picture:

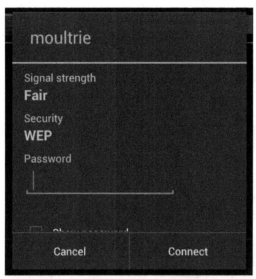

Type in the password and single tap the "Connect" button. Your Device will then connect to the access point. When the Device has successfully connected, you should see this icon on the notification bar. To go back to the settings menu, single tap the back button. Another thing you can do this menu is that if you have possession of a wireless Bluetooth earpiece that looks similar to the next picture:

You can connect (Or Pair) your Bluetooth earpiece to your device within this menu. To do that, you will have to have your Bluetooth antennas turned on. And to do that, single tap the "Off" label on the Bluetooth section to turn the Bluetooth feature on. When the Bluetooth antennas are turned on, read the instructions of your particular earpiece on how to set it to pairing mode. Then single tap the Bluetooth menu choice. When you do that, your screen should look like the next picture:

Your device will then start scanning for nearby Bluetooth devices to pair to and list them in this menu as shown in the next picture:

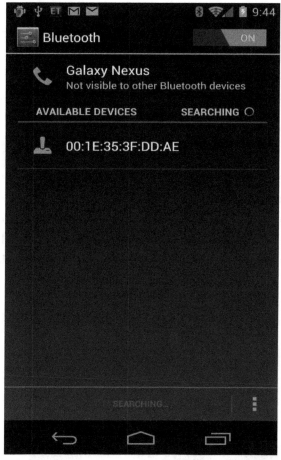

Single tap the device listed in this menu to pair it with this device.

Note – For most earpieces, the pairing password should be the same and the device should take care of the pairing. But if your password is different, then the device will ask you for the password to the earpiece. Then you would use the touch keyboard to enter the password and then you should be all set. To go back to the main settings menu, just single tap the back button .

After setting up desired devices to connect to your phone, you can quickly turn on and off services such as Wi-Fi and Bluetooth by swiping the toggle switches to the right to turn it on or to the left to turn it off. This also helps conserve battery. But a new option in Android 4 (3G & 4G tablets & smartphones only) is the ability to set data usage limits to prevent overages on many wireless carriers new metered or capped data plans.

Wireless carriers went to metered or capped data plans to help reduce network congestion (which leads to dropped calls, very slow internet connections and other issues) and to have users that use a lot of data become more mindful about how much data they use. Single tap the "Data Usage" option and the Usage menu will come up similar to the next picture:

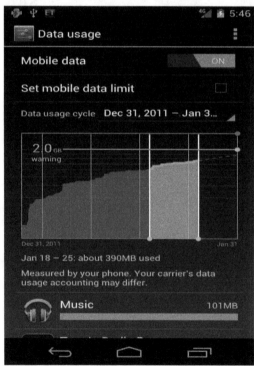

In this section, you can turn the data antenna on your device completely off or on by left or right swiping the Mobile Data toggle switch, or single tapping the "Set mobile data limit" option to turn on data monitoring. When you single tap this checkmark, a prompt letting you know that Data usage monitored by this program and your wireless carrier may differ prompt will come up as shown in the next picture:

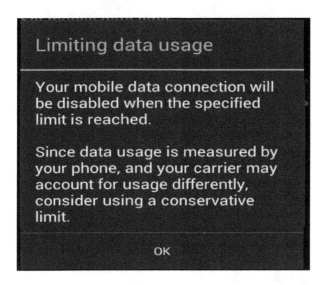

Single tap the "OK" button to enable this feature. Then you will see two lines that are displayed "Warning" and "Limit" as shown in the next picture:

When enabled, your device will give you a notification warning when you are approaching the warning limit setting and totally shut down data capabilities when you reach your maximum data limit so that you will not incur any overage charges. Also in this menu, you can swipe down and up to view every program that is using any data and monitor exactly how much data that particular program is using at any given time.

To set a warning limit, swipe up or down the yellow line to the GB level you wish the phone to warn you. Then the phone will display a warning notification when you approach this limit. To set a max limit, swipe up or down the red line to the GB level you wish. I would suggest setting this line to the maximum limit your particular carriers data plan allows. Your device will automatically disable data transfer & downloads when total data used on your device reaches this limit. To disable this option, just single tap the "Set mobile data limit" checkbox to uncheck it and data limit monitoring will be disabled. To go back to the settings menu, single tap the back button which looks like this 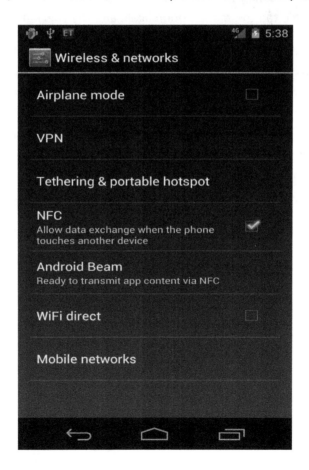, and you will be back to the settings menu. On the settings menu, the last option under the "Wireless & Networks" section is the "More.." option. Single tap on this option, and the screen will come up similar to the next picture:

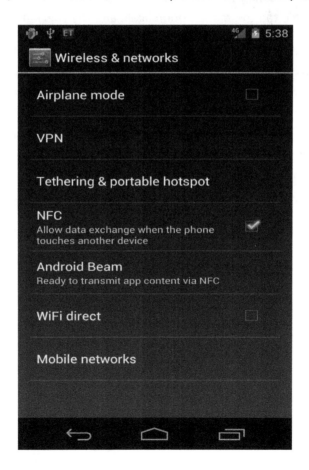

There are many options on this menu and the menu choices and phrases that are used may be new to you, so I am going to explain what they mean and why you should know about them.

Airplane Mode – AKA "offline", "radios off", or "standalone" mode. This is a special "flight" or "airplane" mode that turns off just the wireless radio parts of the device, for safe use on an airplane where radio transmitters are not allowed. To set your Device on Airplane mode, single tap the "Airplane Mode" menu choice, and a green check mark should show indicating that Airplane mode is active. To turn Airplane Mode off, single tap the menu option again and the check mark will go away.

Tethering Mode –This mode allows you to turn your Android device into a Wi-Fi hotspot to connect your laptop to your phone through to use the 3G/4G internet connection from your device. For it to work, you would need to have your wireless carrier enable this function on your device. Of course there is an additional monthly charge for this capability. Single tap on this option, and the tethering mode menu will come up as shown in the next picture:

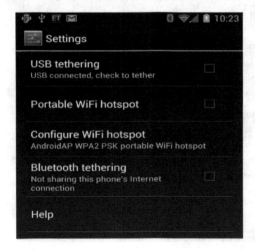

NFC & Android Beam Mode – Android Beam is an innovative, convenient feature for sharing between two Android 4 devices. It lets you instantly exchange favorite apps, contacts, music, videos — almost anything. It's incredibly simple and convenient to use. Make sure that the NFC option on this menu is check marked by single tapping on it to enable it. Then after that, open up the app, video or anything else on one phone you want to send to another.

Then touch one Android-powered phone to another as shown in the next picture:

A prompt menu will come up requesting you to touch the screen to "beam" that item to the other device as shown in the next picture:

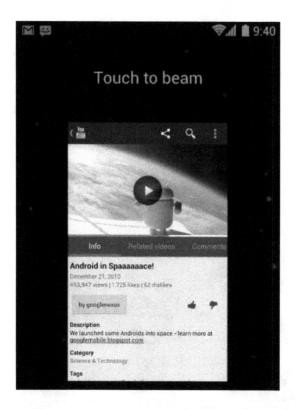

Then single tap the screen to send the video or other content to the other device.

Wi-Fi Direct Mode –Wi-Fi Direct mode lets users connect directly to nearby peer devices over Wi-Fi, for more reliable, higher-speed communication. No internet connection or tethering is needed. Through third-party apps, users can connect to compatible devices to take advantage of new features such as instant sharing of files, photos, or other media; streaming video or audio from another device; or connecting to compatible printers or other devices.

Adding People And Phone Numbers To Your Device

To add people to your address book on your device, Single tap the launch icon from the main screen (You would get to the main screen by pressing the home key on your device. It will look like the following

picture) Single tap the launch icon and swipe left or right to find the People application. Single tap the People app icon and the screen will come up looking like the next picture:

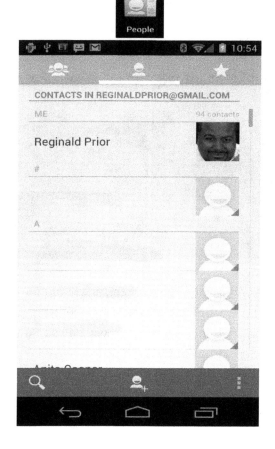

To enter a new contact, single tap the "New" button in the bottom-center part of the screen which looks like this: 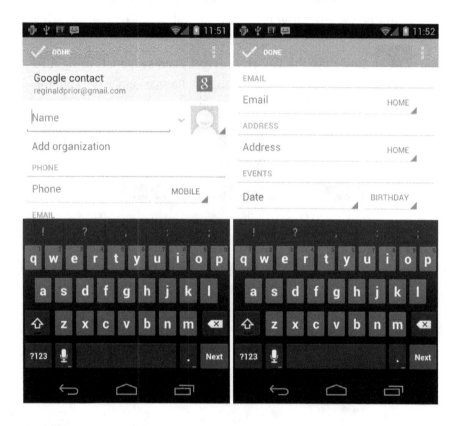 and the add new contact form will come up and look like the picture shown below:

To enter information for your new contact, single tap the "Name" field and then the touch keyboard will come up. Type in the first and name of your contact in this field, then swipe up slowly and single tap each field and fill in information you currently have on this person.

A Couple of Notes –

- You are not limited to entering just the basic type of information for this user. You can add additional information for this contact like their E-Mail addresses, Their Home and Business Addresses and other type of information.

- To add more than one phone number, address or any other kind of information for this contact, locate the "Add New" option as shown in the next picture:

EMAIL

tes   HOME   ✕

Add new

Single tap that option, and another line will show up allowing you to add additional information. You do have the option to change the label under this menu for this and any other additional lines you add to this person's contact information. Say for example, you have just entered the home phone number of this person and want to add the work number also. Notice when you single tapped the "Add New" option, a new line comes up showing "Mobile".

For the label to be correct for this contacts work number, you have to change this field to "Work". To make that change, single tap the down arrow which would look like the following picture ◢ , then the label options menu will come up as shown in the picture below:

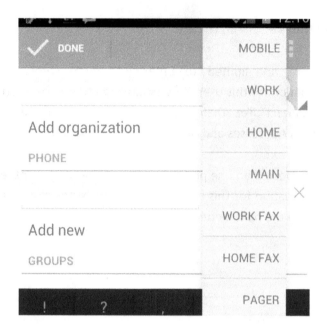

Then single tap the "Work" label. The label for that text field will be changed to "Work". Then single tap the newly created work field and enter the work number. When you are finished entering all of the information for this person, single tap the "Done" button at the upper left of the screen, and all of their information you have entered will now be saved on your device.

Deleting Contacts Off Your Device

To delete a contact from your contact list, Single tap the People Apps icon from the launch screen (You would get to the main screen by pressing the home key on your Device. It will look like the following picture ) single tap the launch icon and swipe left or right to find the People application. Single tap the icon. The main screen will come up similar to the next picture:

Swipe up or down to find the contact that you want to delete from the device. Single tap the contact to pull up that person. The contact screen would look similar to the next picture:

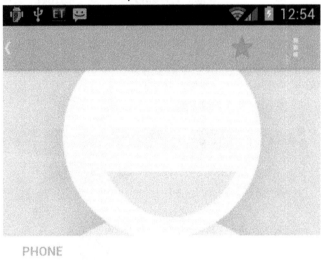

Then press the menu button located at the top-right part of the Device.

It would look like this 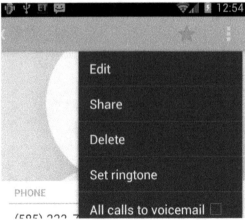 the options menu will come up as shown in the next picture:

To delete this contact, single tap the "Delete" option. A dialog box will come up stating that this contact will be deleted as shown in the next picture:

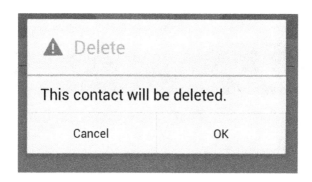

Single tap the "OK" button and the contact will be deleted from your Device.

How To Get Onto The Internet

One of the best aspects about having a smartphone or Device is the ability to surf the internet just about the same way as you would on a computer or a laptop from anywhere. In the past, you would get the Mobile or condensed versions of websites because the browsers on those devices couldn't handle the layouts of those webpages. But the Android 4's web browser app shows websites in their full glory.

To go onto the Internet, You will have to launch the browser application. You will do that by Single tapping the browser icon from the home screen (You would get to the main screen by pressing the home key on your Device. It look like this⬜) Single tap the browser app icon. That icon looks like the next picture:

The Android web browser will come up like the next picture:

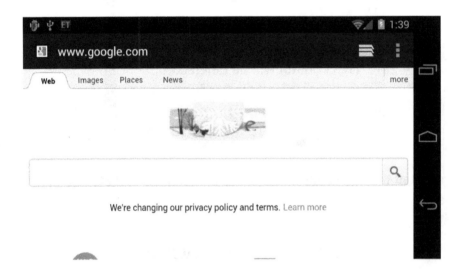

To bring up the address bar so that you can go to a different webpage other than the one that comes up by default, swipe down to go to the top of the current webpage, and the address bar will come up as shown in the next picture:

Single tap inside the address bar and then the touch keyboard will show up where you can type the address of the webpage you wish to go to. While you are typing in the webpage address, a live Google search is being conducted behind the scenes were your desired website may come up. You can single tap on that address if it does come up. An example of this happening is shown on the next picture:

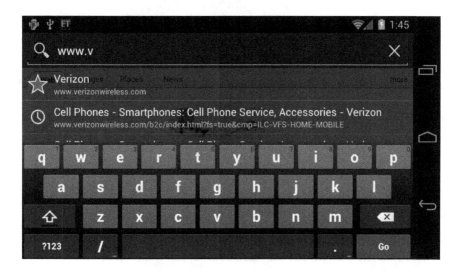

When you are done typing in the desired website, then single tap the blue "Go" button, and you will be taken to that webpage. Just like the browser on your computer, you can set various options such as setting the default webpage among other things.

To show the browser options, while having the Android browser open, press the menu key on your Device at the top right part of the screen which looks like this [icon]. The option menu will come up like the next picture.

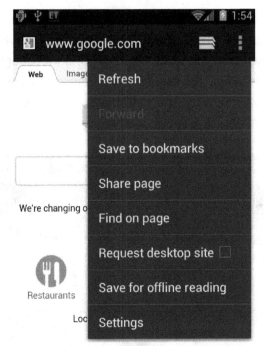

From here, you can do things such as saving this website to your bookmarks, or setting the default website that shows when the browser opens. To do that, single tap the "Settings" option. The screen will come up looking similar to the next picture:

To change the default website, single tap the "General" option and the set General options screen will come up like the next picture:

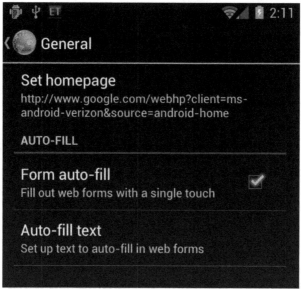

To change the homepage, single tap the "Set Homepage" option and the set homepage screen will come up similar to the next picture:

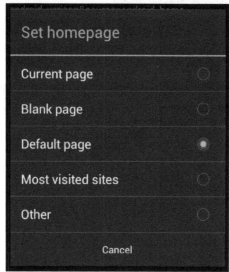

You can easily set the homepage to the current website that is up currently by single tapping the current page option, or is you want to type it in manually, single tap the "Other" option. The screen to manually enter the website you want to set as the default will come up similar to the next picture:

Type in the desired website you wish to come up first and single tap the "OK" button and the new default webpage will be set to the page you enter in that text area.

<u>Using Tabs To Navigate Multiple Websites (For Smartphones)</u>

Another thing you can do in Android 4's web browser is to navigate multiple websites using tabs. To manage tabs, single tap the tabs icon which looks like this 🔲. When you do that, the tabs menu will come up similar to the next picture:

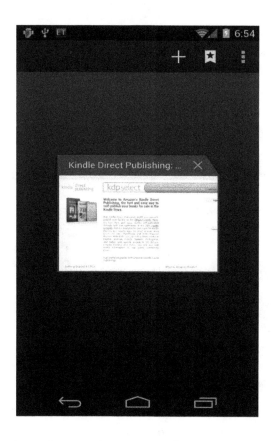

To create another tab to navigate to a different website, single tap the

plus symbol which looks like this and a new tab will be created and
the web browser will go to the default webpage. Then you would go to
your other webpage you wish to go to. To view all of your open tabs,

single tap the taps icon , and all of your open tabs will show similar
to the next picture:

You can swipe up or down to navigate through all of your active tabs. To close a tab, single tap the "X" icon at the top right of the tab. Then the tab will be removed from this list. To go to a particular tab, just single tap on it and the web browser will then go to that tab.

Using Tabs To Navigate Multiple Websites (For Tablets)

To create another tab to navigate to a different website on a tablet, single tap the plus symbol which looks like this ✚ and a new tab will be created.

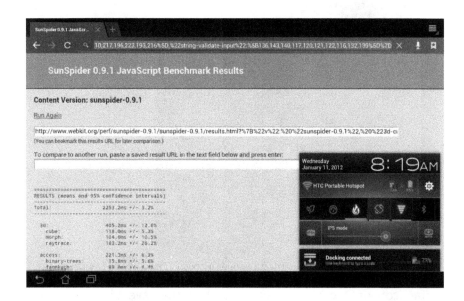

Then you would single tap in the address bar, type in the other webpage you wish to go to, then single tap the "Go" button on your touch keyboard. To go to a particular tab, just single tap on it and the web browser will then go to that tab. To close a tab, single tap the "X" icon at the top right of the tab. Then the tab will be removed from the web browser.

Bookmarking Favorite Webpages

You can also create bookmarks in the Android 4 web browser. To bookmark a webpage, first go to the website you wish to bookmark, then single tap the menu icon ⦙ in the address bar. When you do this, your screen will look similar to the next picture:

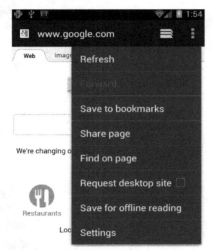

then single tap the "Save to Bookmarks" option. On a tablet, single tap the star icon on the address bar ⭐, then the save to bookmarks prompt will come up similar to the next picture:

Single tap the "OK" button and your bookmark is now added to your web browsers bookmarks list. To view all of your bookmarks, single tap the tabs button to the right of the address bar which would look similar to this icon ▤. The tabs menu will come up looking similar to the next picture:

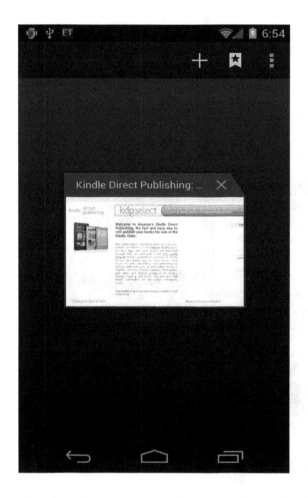

To view your bookmarks, on a smartphone, single tap the bookmark ribbon 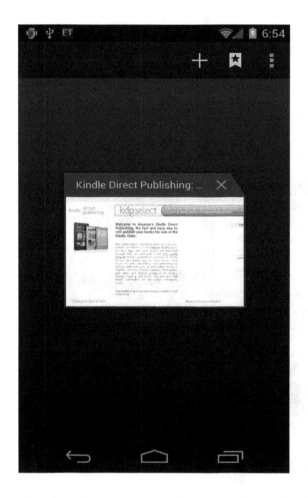 under the tabs menu, and all of your bookmarks will show up in a list as shown in the next picture:

For tablets, on the main browser screen, just single tap the bookmark ribbon ▨ to be taken to your bookmarks. To go to a specific bookmark, single tap the specific bookmark and the browser will then go to that website.

How To Setup And Use E-Mail

Electronic Mail or E-Mail has forever changed how people communicate from the business world, to families that live far away so that they can easily stay in touch. E-Mail allows you not only to send letters to people, but also you can send pictures and other things.

Note – If you have a Gmail account, you can use that account with your Device for E-Mail. But if you want to use an email account from your Internet Service Provider for your home computers, you can use that account also with your Android device.

But before we get into using your email account on your Android device, first we would have to Configure Android Mail to work with the E-Mail address your Internet Service Provider has given you to use. The 4 things we will need to get your E-Mail to work are listed below:

1. Your Internet Service POP Server address (POP stands for Post Office Protocol). It handles E-Mail coming in from people that has sent you E-Mail.

2. Your Internet Service SMTP Server address (SMTP stands for Simple Mail Transfer Protocol). This is used to send messages and forwards that you have written to people.

3. The username you gave the Internet service provider to setup your Internet account with them.

4. Also the password that you gave the Internet service provider to setup your Internet account with them.

If you don't remember or lost the documentation that they gave to you, you are going to have to call the customer service of the Internet Service Provider that you using to get this information, because you are going to need it to get Android Mail® to send and receive E-Mails at all. When you have this information, we can move on to the next step: setting up the e-mail program itself.

To setup the e-mail account for your Internet Service Provider, Single tap the launch icon from the main screen (You would get to the main screen by pressing the home key on your Device. It look like this ⬠) and swipe left or right to find the Android Mail application. Single tap the Android Mail® app, which icon looks like the next picture

Email

The Email Application will come up and your screen should look like the next picture:

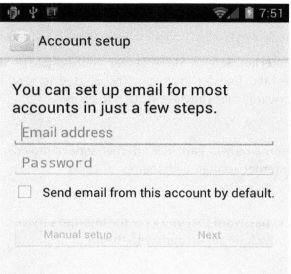

This screen is the first step in the Android Mail® wizard where they ask you to type in e-mail address and your password in the text boxes. Single tap the Email Address box, And the touch keyboard comes up. Type in the e-mail address your Internet Service Provider has given you. It is usually <u>username@internetprovidername.com</u> .org or .net.

Then single tap the password box, type in your password, then single tap the "Next" button on the Device screen.

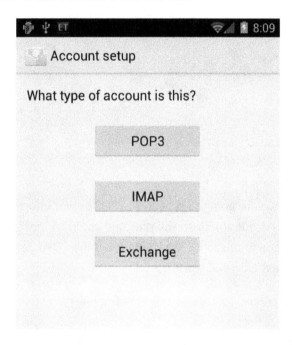

This screen is the step where they ask you to specify the type of email that you are using. In most cases, it would be POP mail, so single tap the "POP" button.

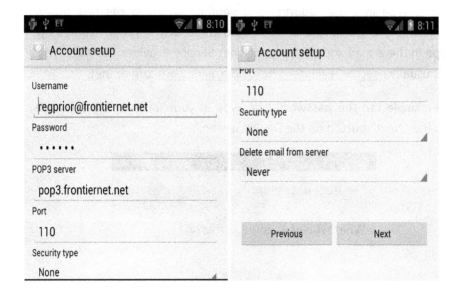

In this window, we are going to type in the POP server information from your Internet Service Provider so the program could connect to the right servers to deliver and to send E-Mail. Single tap the POP3 Server textbox and the touch keyboard will come up.

Type your pop server address in the POP3 server box, then single tap the password text field, type in your password and swipe up to go to the end of this menu, then single tap the "Next" button.

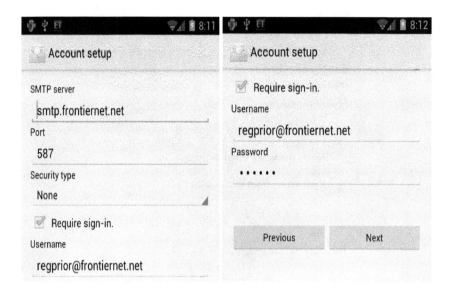

In this window, we are going to type in the SMTP server information from your Internet Service Provider. Single tap the SMTP Server textbox and the touch keyboard will come up.

Type your server address in the SMTP server box, then single tap the password text field and type in your password, and swipe up to go to the end of this menu, then single tap the "Next" button.

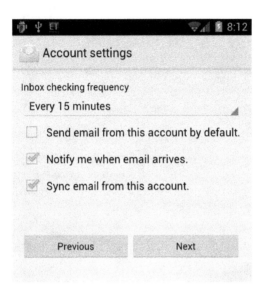

This screen shows additional options you can set for this email account such as notifications and the different intervals that the device will check for new email messages. Single tap the desired boxes if you want to change the default options set here, otherwise single tap the "Next" button.

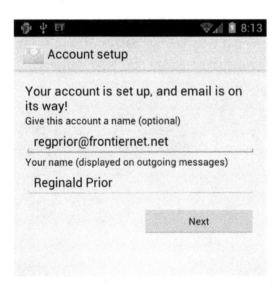

This screen is where you can set up a specialized name for this E-Mail box. Also in this menu, you would type in your name or a name you want people to see when they receive emails you send from this Device. Fill in this information and single tap the "Next" button.

Your Android device will now attempt to connect to the email service using the information you typed in. And if the attempt was successful, then the program will start downloading email as shown in the next picture:

And your email is now setup and ready to go!

Sending E-Mail From Your Device

To send email using your Device, you would have to go back into Android Mail by single tapping the launch icon from the main screen (You would get to the main screen by pressing the home key on your Device. It look like this ▢) and swipe left or right to find the Android Mail application. Single tap the icon that looks like the next picture:

And the Android Mail app will load and check for new Emails and will look like the next picture:

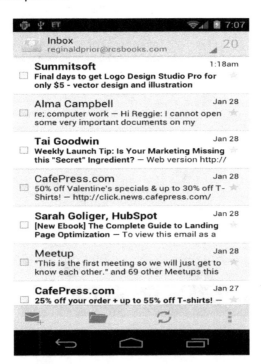

To start composing a new email message, Single tap the "Compose" icon located in the lower left part of the screen which looks like this  the new message window will then come up and looks similar to the next picture

To create a message, have the person's e-mail handy. Make sure the spelling of the e-mail is correct because your message will not be sent at all if the spelling is incorrect. The steps below are how you would compose the e-mail in Android mail

1. First, single tap the "To:" textbox. The touch screen keyboard will come up. Type the e-mail address of the person that you want to send this message to in the textbox. Again, make sure that the e-mail address is correctly spelled, or the message will not be sent at all.

2. Secondly, single tap the "Subject:" textbox. Type a brief summary of what this e-mail is about in the textbox.

3. Thirdly, single tap the compose mail textbox on the bottom of the window. Type the actual message in this box.

4. Lastly, you can attach a photo from your device by single tapping the options button at the top right part of the screen which looks like this 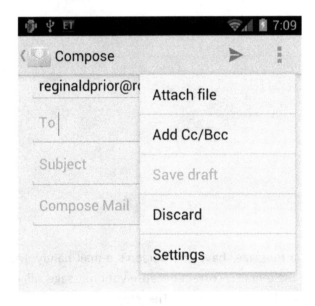 and the email options will come up similar to the next picture:

Single tap the "Attach File" option and you will be taken to your picture gallery as shown in the next picture:

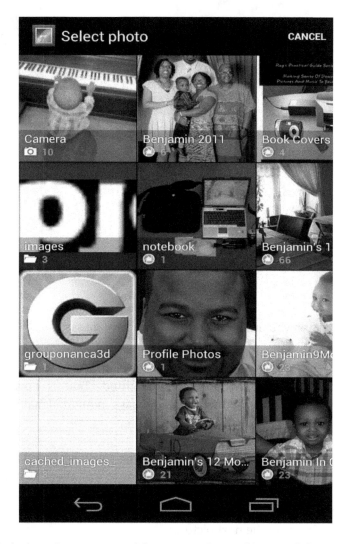

Find the picture you wish to attach to this email by single tapping one of the albums listed here, then find the picture you wish to attach by swiping left or right in the album then single tapping the picture to attach it to this email message as shown in the next picture:

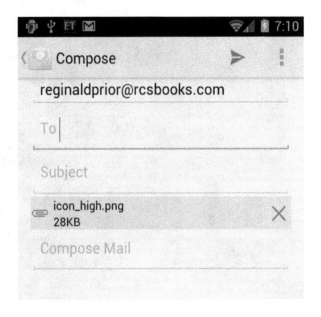

5. When you are done typing your actual message to this recipient of this message, single tap the send button in the upper right part of this screen. Your E-Mail message will then be sent to the e-mail address you inputted. That is how you put together and send an e-mail message in Android mail.

Note – notice on the bottom left part of the touch keyboard next to the space bar, you will notice a microphone icon that looks like this: This button will activate the speech to text feature of Android. Single tap this button and the speech to text feature will start and look similar to the next picture:

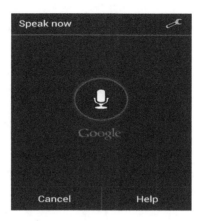

When this dialog box appears, just speak to your phone in your natural voice and the phone will convert what you say to text, freeing you from typing with the touch keyboard. Wherever you see this icon, you can utilize the speech to text feature of your Android phone.

Deleting Messages In Android Mail

To delete a message in Android Mail, Single tap the apps icon from the main screen (You would get to the main screen by pressing the home key on your device. It look like this ⬜) and swipe up or down to find the Android Mail application. Single tap the Android mail icon that looks like the next picture:

On the main screen, swipe up or down to find the message(s) you wish to delete, and single tap the square box to the left of the message(s) you wish to delete. It would now look similar to the next picture:

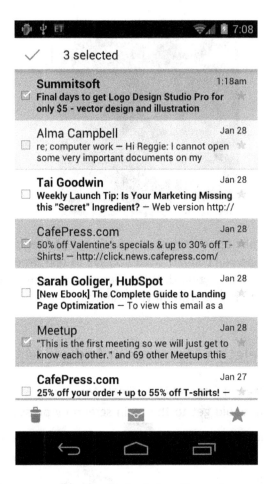

To delete this message(s), simply single tap the garbage can icon located

at the bottom left part of the screen which would look like this 🗑

and the message (s) will be deleted from your device.

Using The Camera To Take Pictures And Video

Another thing that you can do with your Android Device is to use it as a camera to take photo pictures or as a camcorder to shoot videos. Depending on the size of your memory card in your Device, you can take lots of pictures or shoot hours of video. To get started taking pictures, Single tap the apps icon from the main screen (You would get to the main screen by pressing the home key on your Device. It look like this) Swipe left or right to find the Camera application. Single tap the Camera app icon that looks like the picture shown below:

The camera program will come up and will look similar to the next picture:

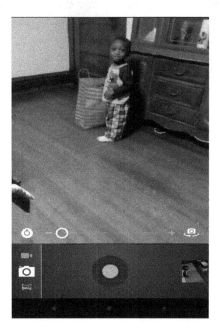

To take a picture, simply just point your Device at whatever it is you want to take the picture of and single tap the blue shutter icon which looks like this

And the camera will focus itself and then take the picture and save the picture to your Devices memory card.

Note – Most Android devices now come with front-facing cameras which can be used to take pictures of yourself also. To activate the front-facing camera, single tap the camera switch icon which would look like this: The camera will then switch and then you can single tap the shutter icon to take a picture of yourself.

Another thing you can do with your Android device is to shoot video like a camcorder. Depending on the size of your memory card in your Device, you can take quite a bit of video.

To shoot videos, single tap the section on the bottom left where you see three icons that look similar to the next picture:

Then the device will slide out the three selection icons like the next picture:

Then single tap the camcorder icon to switch to turn your device to "Camcorder Mode". The device will turn to camcorder mode and look like the next picture:

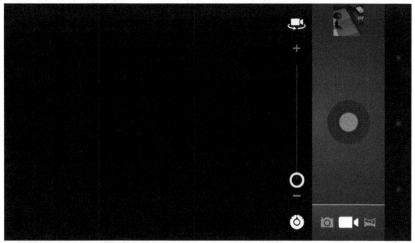

To start shooting video, single tap the red record button. It looks like this. The Device is now recording video to your devices memory card. To stop taking video, single tap the stop button. That button would look like this . Your Device will stop recording video and save the video on your memory card.

Note – Most Android Devices come with a front-facing webcam which can be used to take video of yourself also. To activate the front-facing camera, single tap the camcorder switch icon which would look like this: The camera will then switch and then you can single tap the red record icon to record a video of yourself.

How To Download Pictures To Your Device

Most people have pictures on their computer that they may want to show to other people or view from time to time. You could get one of those keychain digital photo frames that look like the next picture:

But the truth of the matter is that the quality of the pictures downloaded to the frame leaves a lot to be desired and also the software on some of them that are used to download pictures to them are not the easiest to use.

The more logical solution is to use your Android device as a portable picture frame. The way to download pictures off of your computer to your Android device cannot be any simpler than the instructions we are about to get into now. To transfer your pictures from your computer to your Android device, you will have to use a service called Picasa's Web Albums. Open your computers web browser and go to http://picasaweb.google.com and the webpage will come up looking like the next picture:

At this screen, enter your Gmail E-Mail address and password and single left click the "Sign In" button to log into the service. Picasa Web Albums is a free service that allows you to upload and easily share your photos in many different ways including syncing with your Android devices, which we about to do now.

After you have signed into Picasa Web Albums, the webpage will then open up to the main screen that will similar to the next picture:

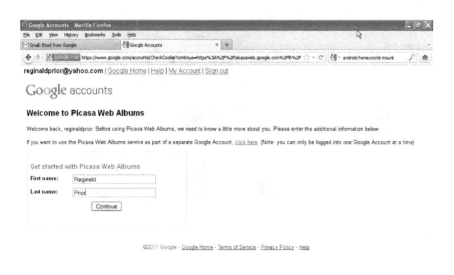

Since this is the first time you are using your Gmail account to sign into the Picasa Web Albums service, you will have to fill out some information before you can use the service. This screen is where you would enter your first and last name and single left click the "Continue" button.

At this screen, you would have to create a Google Profile so that you can have access to all Google's other services including syncing your photos to your Android tablet or cell phone if you have one already. Single left click the "Yes, Create my Google Profile" button and you will be done setting up your online photo album and will come to the main screen as shown in the next picture:

To upload pictures to Picasa Web Albums to sync with your Android device, single left click the "Upload" button and the screen will come up requesting you create an album to upload picture(s) into. It would look similar to the next picture:

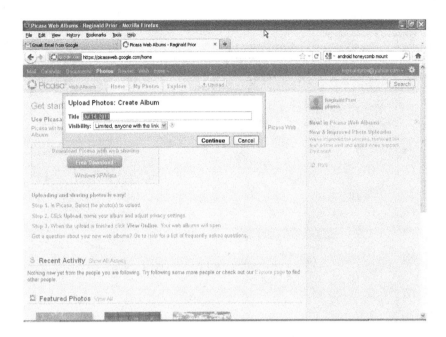

Type in this textbox a name that clearly describes the photos you are planning to upload into this album and single left click the "Continue" button.

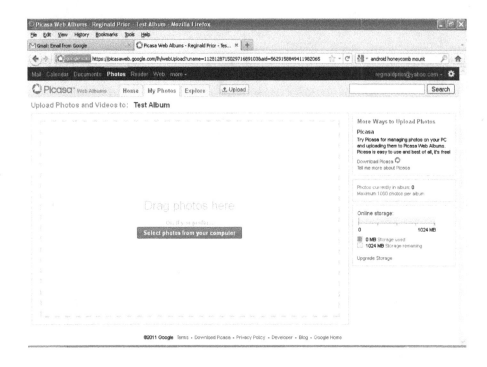

To transfer pictures to this newly created album, single left click the "Select Photos From Your Computer" button in the middle of the screen, and the upload picture box will come up as shown in the next picture:

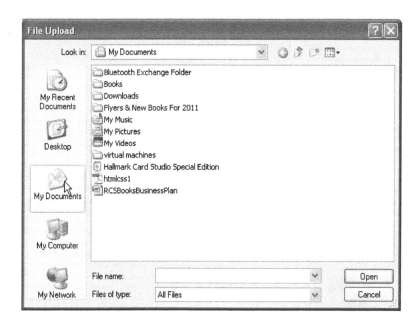

Select the picture that you want to upload from your computer to this album in this box. Usually pictures download into the "My Pictures" folder. You would get to this folder by single left clicking the "My Documents" button on the far left of this window, then double left click on the "My pictures" folder and they should come up.

Find the picture you wish to upload to this album and single left click that picture and then the "Open" button. That picture will then be uploaded to Picasa Web Albums and show up similar to the next picture:

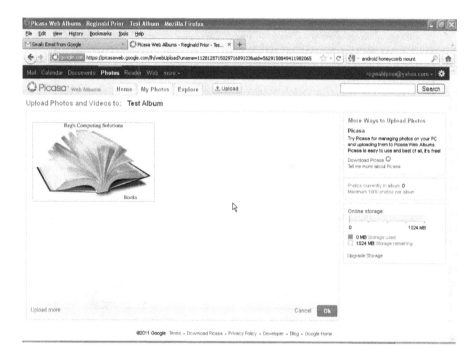

At this point, the picture was successfully uploaded. Then go through the rest of your albums and select other pictures you wish sync and upload them the same way. You can then single left click the "Home" option to take you back to the main screen, where you will see all of the albums you have created.

When you are done uploading all of the pictures to Picasa web albums that you want to view on your Android device, single tap the gallery app in the launch menu from the home screen which icon looks like the next picture:

And the pictures should sync up where you can single tap on them to show up full screen on your device as shown in the next picture with the Picasa logo next to each album. I previously had uploaded a folder called "Benjamin6Mos" to my Device, as you can see it below in the gallery.

Single tap on that album, and all the pictures in that album would show up on the screen. You can show your downloaded pictures in a slideshow by single tapping a slide show icon in the upper right part of the screen which would look similar to this ▶. Your pictures in that album will then show in a slideshow.

Note – You can press the back button anytime during the slide show to end the slide show.

Using The Gallery To Delete Pictures And Video

There are times when you want to remove a picture or video clip from your Device to free up memory on your Device. To delete a picture or video clip from your Device, open the Gallery app from the apps menu from the main screen (You would get to the main screen by pressing the home key on your Device. It look like this) swipe left or right to find the gallery app as shown in the next picture.

Single tap the icon and your pictures will show up where you can left or right swipe in the gallery and single tap a album to show pictures as shown in the next picture.

To delete a picture or video clip on your Device, first open the album where the picture is located by swiping left or right through that gallery and single tapping the album to show all of the pictures in the album as shown in the next picture:

To select a picture to delete, single tap the picture to bring it up full screen. At the top right part of the screen, you will notice a garbage can icon which looks like this: single tap that icon and a menu will come up asking you to confirm deleting this picture as shown in the next picture

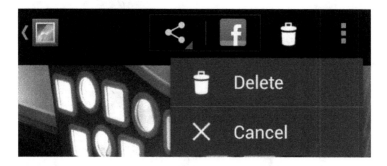

Single tap the "Confirm Delete" button and the picture will be deleted from your Device.

How To Download Music To Your Device

The first thing you will have to do to download music to your Device is to plug one end of the usb cable that came with your Device into your Device and the other end into your computer. Then your computer will show your Device as a mtp device as shown in the next picture:

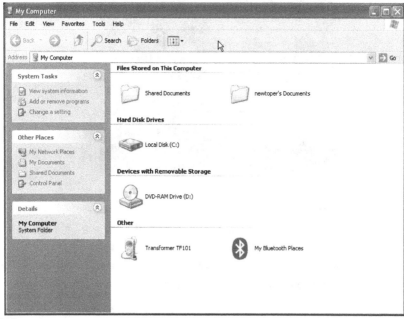

But before we can transfer music to your Android Device, we first would have to download music from your music CD's to your computer. And to do that, get your favorite music CD's together to import into your computer.

Open up Windows Media Player to the main screen and insert one of your music CD's into your computer. Windows Media Player will read the CD and the songs from the CD will appear in the song list section of the program as shown in the next picture:

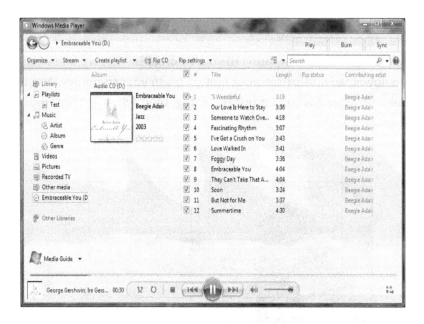

The next step to transferring a music CD to your computer is first making sure that Windows Media Player transfers the music to your computer into the MP3 format. This format is most compatible with your Device.

And how to do that depends on which version of Windows Media Player you have installed on your computer. In Windows Media Player 11, which is installed for Windows XP and Vista, move your mouse cursor to the down arrow under the "Rip" button and single left click on it. A submenu will show up as shown in the picture below.

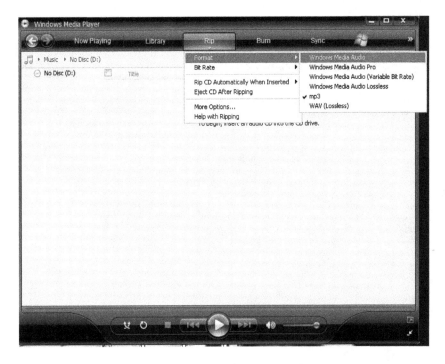

Windows Media Player 11 Screen

Under the format submenu, make sure you have the MP3 format check marked as shown in the previous picture. With Windows Media Player Version 12, which is only for Windows 7 at the time of the writing of this book, single left click the "Rip Settings" button. Under the format submenu, make sure you have the MP3 format check marked as shown in the next picture:

Windows Media Player 12 Screen

After that, single left click the CD icon on the library section of Windows Media Player. The songs on the CD will appear in the songs list section with a check mark next to each one of them. If you want all of the songs on this CD to be transferred to the computer, leave the check marks there. If not, uncheck the songs you don't want to transfer by single left clicking the check mark of each song to unselect them from the transfer list.

When you're ready to download the music CD, single left click the "Rip" button. Then the music will be downloaded to your computer. Repeat the last instructions for each additional CD you want to import into your computer to transfer to your Device.

The next step in the process to play your music on your Android Device is to actually transfer music from your computer to your Device. And to do that, first single left click the arrow next to the music menu in the Library section on the main menu. A submenu will come up with three choices, Artist, Album & Genre. Single left click on Artist.

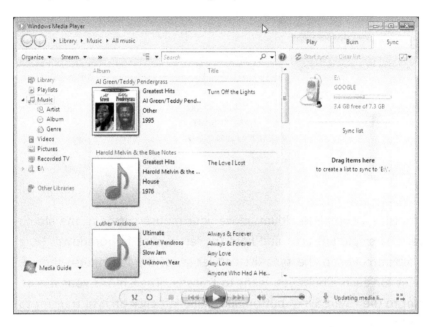

All of the music that you have downloaded onto your computer will come up in the song list section, arranged by Artist. Double left click an artist to show songs and individual albums you have from that artist on your computer. To transfer an individual song to your Device, move your mouse cursor to the song and single left click and hold the left mouse button down.

Drag the song to the sync list where it says "Drag Items Here" and let go of the left mouse button. Repeat for each song you want to transfer. Then move your mouse cursor to the "Start Sync" button and single left click on it to transfer the music to your Device.

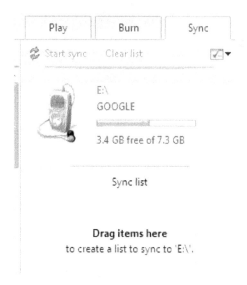

Play	Burn	Sync

Start sync   Clear list

E:\
GOOGLE

3.4 GB free of 7.3 GB

Sync list

Drag items here
to create a list to sync to 'E:\'.

To transfer a complete album, move your mouse cursor to the album cover and single left click and hold the left mouse button down. Drag the album cover to the sync list and let go of the left mouse button. Repeat for each album you want to transfer. Then move your mouse cursor to the "Start Sync" button and single left click on it to transfer to your Android Device.

When you are done copying all of the music that you want to your Device, disconnect the USB cable from your computer and then the music transferred to your Device will be ready for playing.

Using The Music App To View And Play Your Music

In the previous section, "How to Download Music to Your Device" we went over how to transfer music from your personal CD's to your computer and from there, onto your Device. Now you want to play
116

them on your Device. You would do that using the music app. It is under the launch menu located on the main screen. You would get to the main screen by pressing the home key on your Device. It looks similar to this), After you get to the home screen, single tap the launch icon swipe left or right until you see the icon which icon looks like the next picture:

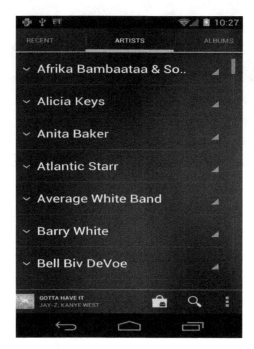

And the music that you downloaded to your Device should show up where you can single tap on them to play on your Device as shown in the next picture.

To see the song list from a particular artist, single tap that artist's name. In this case, I will tap the artist Barry White. Then all of the albums that I have downloaded from Barry White will come up as shown in the next picture:

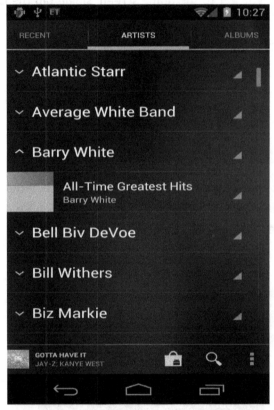

Then to see the songs from a particular album, single tap the album and the song list will show as shown in the next picture:

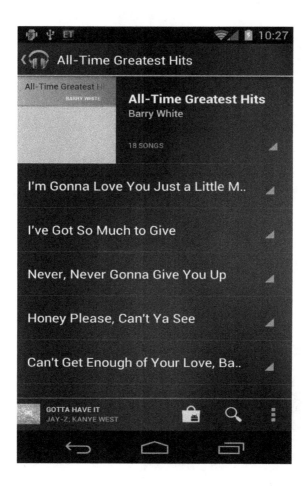

When the song list comes up, you can swipe up or down to view all of the songs and then single tap a song to play it. When you do that, your screen will look like the next picture:

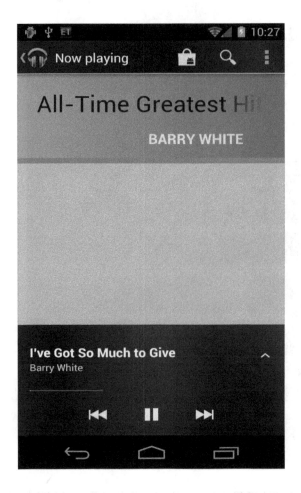

On this screen, you can rewind, pause and go to the next song by tapping on the appropriate buttons. The buttons are shown on the next page:

This button is the pause/play button. When the song is currently playing, this button will turn to the pause symbol. When a song is paused, then this button will turn to the play symbol.

 This button is to cycle to the next song on The current play list.

This button is to go back to the previous song on the play list.

To go back to the main music screen, press the back button on your Device which looks like this and then you would go back to the song list.

Note – If you want to delete a song from your Device, while under the song list section, press the down arrow key next to the particular song.

It would look similar to this , and the song menu will come up as shown in the next picture.

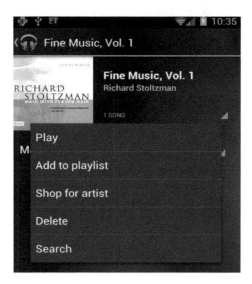

Single tap the "Delete" menu, and a menu prompt will come up making sure that you want to delete this particular song as shown in the next picture:

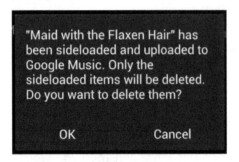

Single tap the "OK" button, and the song will be deleted from your Device.

Chapter Three:

Using The Android Market To Add Functionality To Your Device

Getting To The Android Market

A lot of buzz words have been circulating about mobile devices for a year or so. But the word "Apps" has been a big one for sure. Apps are short for Application and share the same meaning as with regular computers.

Applications are programs designed to perform a function or suite of related functions of benefit to an end user such as email or word processing. On an Android Device, you would get your applications from the Android Market.

To get to the Android Market, on the main screen (You would get to the main screen by pressing the "Home" key on your Device. It would look like this), You should see the Market icon. Single tap the Market Icon which looks like the next picture:

Market

And the Android market main screen will come up looking like the next picture:

Downloading And Installing Apps

To install an app on your Device from the Android Market, there are two ways to do it. The first method is that if you know the name of the app that you want to install, single tap the textbox next to the magnifying glass icon in the upper right part of the screen and the touch screen keyboard will come up like the next picture.

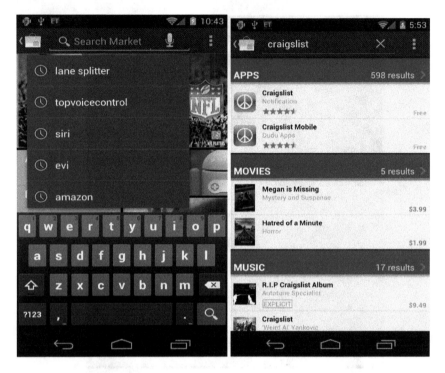

App Search Screen   App Results Screen

Type in the name of the app in the search box and single tap the blue

hourglass icon which looks like this ▨, then the Device will search the
Android market for the app. If the app is available on the market, then it
will show up in the results box where you would single tap on it to go to
the download screen, then single tap the "Accept & Download" button
to install this app on your Device as shown in the next pictures:

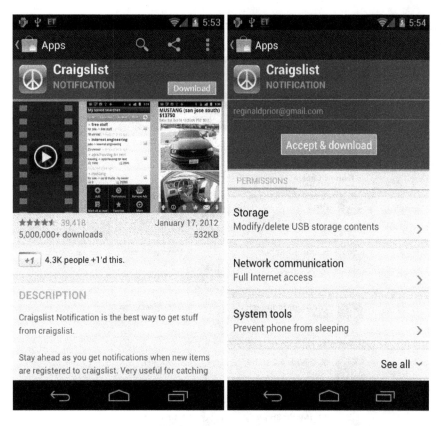

The second way to install apps on your Device is to actually look around on the Android market for apps. Keep in mind that there are millions of apps on the Android market and growing every day.

The easiest way to do that is when you are at the Android Market main screen, on the left side of this screen, you can single tap a specific category and look through that category for an app that way.

For example, if you were curious about the apps in the media & video category, single tap the apps section, then swipe right to see the all of the categories, then swipe up until you see the and all of the media &

video programs that are in the Android market will show up as shown in the next picture:

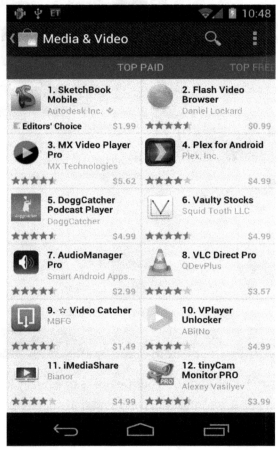

You would swipe up or down or left to right to cycle through free and paid apps. When you come across one that interests you, single tap on it to view a description of the app and the button to install it as shown in the next picture:

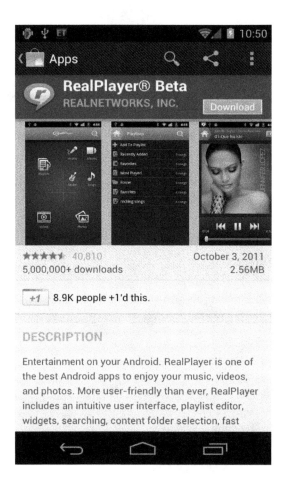

Single tap the download button here, then single tap the "Accept & Download" button to actually download and install this app to your device.

Note – Some apps are free and some are ones that you have to pay for. And the way that you can tell if an app is free or pay is that in on the same line of the app, it would either list "Free" or the cost of the app in US dollars.

And if you install the apps that are not free, you would have to purchase them off your credit card through Google checkout.

Another note about apps – Periodically the companies or persons who created certain apps that you have installed on your Device release updates to these apps. To update them, an update icon will appear on your notification bar with the Android market logo.

Single tap the market icon on the notification bar, and a menu choice would state that they are updates available for your Device. Single tap on that menu choice and all of the updates for the apps will come up as shown in the next picture:

The apps installed on your Device that has an update available will be flagged under the "Update" section. To update that app, single tap on the app and a menu will come up for that particular app. Single tap the update button and another prompt will come up stating that this program will be updated and your existing files will be saved. Single tap the OK button and the app will be updated.

Uninstalling Apps That You Don't Use

From time to time, you may have installed a lot of apps on your Device and would need to clear some space for one reason or another. The best way to clear space on your Device is to remove apps that you don't use that often.

To remove the apps that you don't use often is to go to the main screen (You would get to the main screen by pressing the "Home" key on your Device. It would look like this 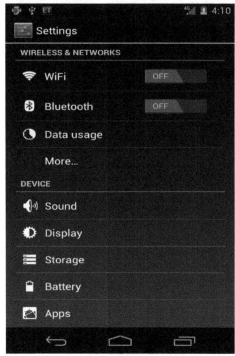), single tap the launch icon on the home screen, then swipe left or right until you see the "Settings" option. Single tap on that and the settings menu will come up like the next picture:

Swipe up until you see the "Apps" option. Single tap that option and all of the apps currently installed on your device will come up similar to the next picture:

To uninstall an app, swipe up or down to find the app that you want to remove and single tap on it to bring up the app details menu as shown in the next picture:

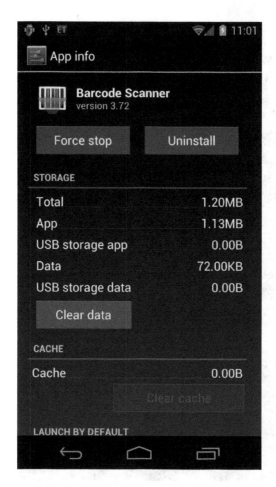

On this menu, single tap the uninstall button and a prompt will come up confirming that you want to uninstall this particular app as shown in the next picture:

Single tap the OK button then the app will be removed from your Device.

Chapter Four:

Device Security

As convenient and easy it is to do many things on your Android Device, the fact remains that Android Devices carry a lot of personal information on them where it could be dangerous if your Device ever gets stolen or someone else who is using your Device does something on an application where it could adversely affect you in one way or another.

Here are some things you can do to lessen your risk of these things to occur.

The first thing you can do to protect your data is to set an unlock pattern for your Device. You would do that by going into the settings menu in the launch menu by going to the main screen (You would get to the main screen by pressing the "Home" key on your Device. It would look like this ⬠)

Single tap the launch button icon and swipe left or right to locate the settings button, which looks like this

Settings

single tap this button and the settings screen will come up like the next picture:

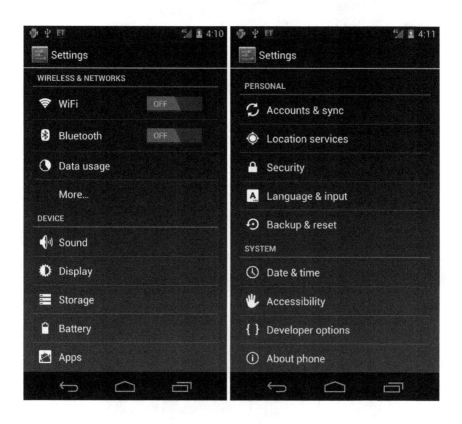

Swipe up until you see the "Security" option. Single tap the security menu option and the screen should look like the next picture:

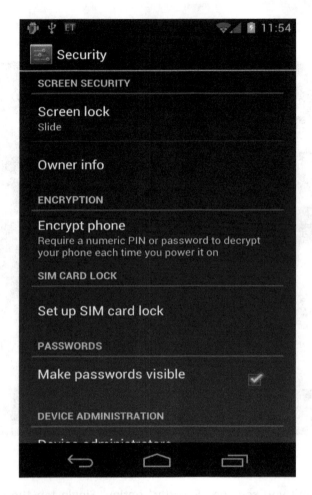

To set a unlock pattern, single tap the "Screen Lock" option and your screen will come up like the next picture:

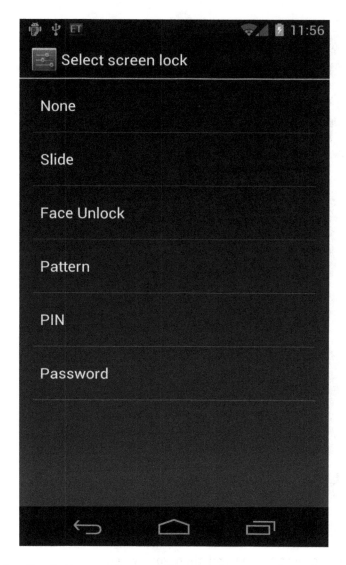

Single tap the Pattern option and the securing your phone intro screen will come up as shown in the next picture:

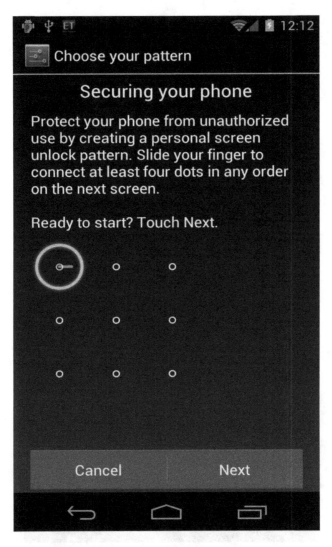

Single tap the next button and then you would use your fingers and draw an unlock pattern as shown in the next picture:

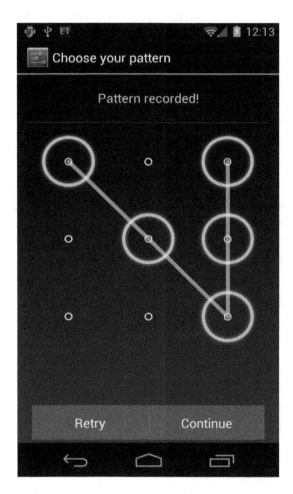

Remember to create a pattern that you can easily remember, because if you forget the pattern, you cannot unlock your Device and would have to go to your carrier to reset your Device which could erase everything on it!!!!

When you have created a pattern, single tap the "continue" button. You will be prompted to draw the same pattern again. Draw the pattern again and single tap the "confirm" button to set the pattern on your Device.

Now your unlock screen will look like the next picture:

If you don't want to keep the unlock pattern and want to swipe in, you would unset the unlock pattern for your Device. You would do that by going into the settings menu in the launch menu by going to the main screen (You would get to the main screen by pressing the "Home" key on your Device. It would look like this )

Single tap the launch button icon and swipe left or right to locate the settings button, which looks like this

single tap this button and the settings screen will come up like the next picture:

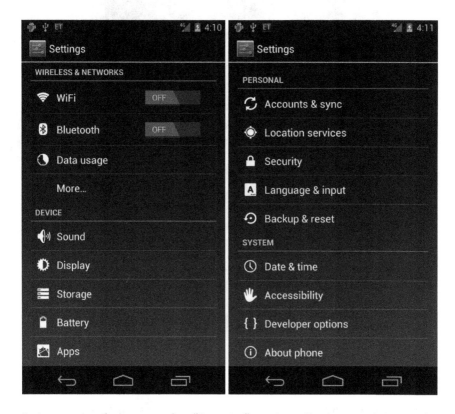

Swipe up until you see the "Security" option. Single tap the security menu option and the screen should look like the next picture:

To unset the screen lock pattern, single tap the "Screen Lock" option and your screen will come up asking you to confirm your saved pattern and go back to the screen lock settings like the next picture(s):

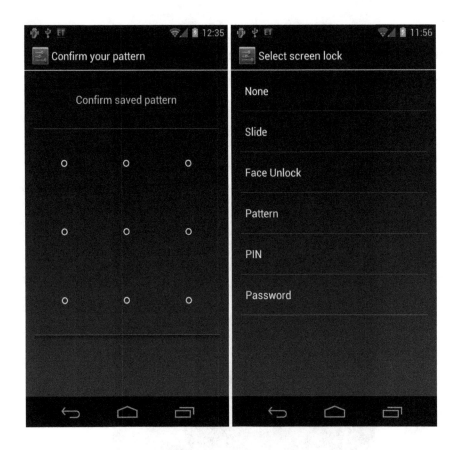

To unset the unlock pattern, single tap the "slide" option to go back to the original unlock settings.

Probably one of the most talked about features in Android 4 the facial recognition unlock feature. The ability to use your own face to unlock your mobile telephone or tablet is one of the coolest new updates we have seen implemented into a operating system in recent times.

To setup this feature on your device, in the security menu under the settings option, single tap the screen lock option, then single tap the face unlock option. Your screen should look similar to the next picture:

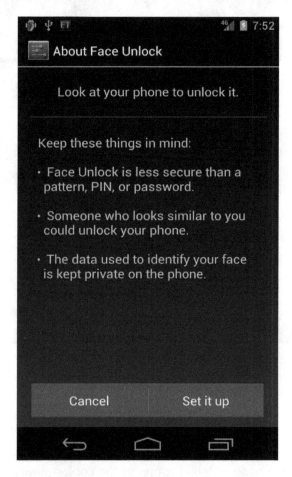

Single tap the "Set it up" option to get started. Then the next step in setting up the face unlock feature will look similar to the next picture:

This screen that comes up gives you a couple of suggestions for recording the best possible picture to unlock your phone. Single tap the "Continue" button to actually take a snapshot of your face as in the next picture:

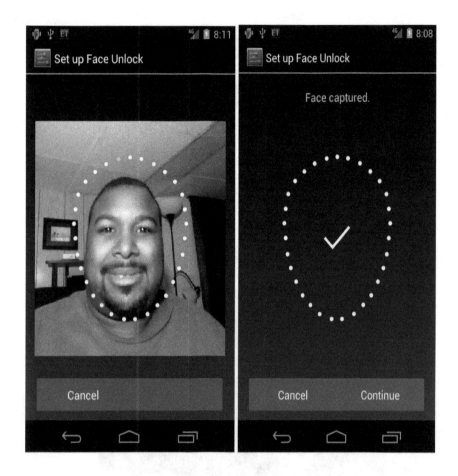

Hold your device to your face and make sure your face is inside the dotted lines. When your phone records a snapshot of your face, then the face captured screen will come up as shown in the previous picture. Single tap the "Continue" button to move on to the next step.

This screen makes you setup an alternative way for unlocking your device just in case the face unlock feature is not working. You can setup a pin code or a pattern to facilitate unlocking your phone. Select one of these options and set that option up to unlock your device. Then you are all done setting up the face unlock feature as shown in the next picture:

149

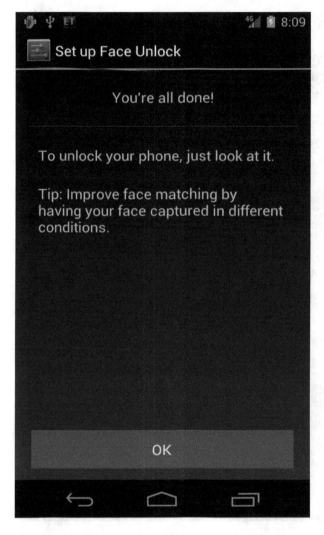

Single tap the "OK" button and you are all set. When you go to unlock your phone, the screen should look like the next picture:

When you hold your device to your face, your device should unlock.

The next measure of device security you should employ is to go to the Android market and install the lookout security app. Then either go to https://www.mylookout.com/ and sign up for an account, or do it through your Android device as shown in the next picture:

This application includes an antivirus, anti-malware program and a backup utility to make sure that you don't lose anything on your device and also locate your device or remotely wipe your phone if your device is lost or stolen so that no one would be able to have access to your information. Keep in mind that lookout comes in two versions, free and premium. The premium features for $29.99 per year include Privacy Advisor and the Safe Browsing tools, which add another level of protection.

We all in the past at one time or another have lost our phone and frantically go looking for it and found that your device was stolen off your person. With lookout installed and active on the phone, you can go online from any Internet connected computer to http://www.mylookout.com, sign into the website and start the process of locating your device as shown in the next picture:

Single left click on the "Log In" button to bring up the login screen:

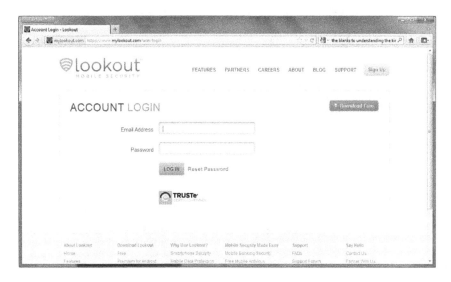

Enter your email address and password you had used to sign up for your lookout account and single left click the "Log In" button. The main screen will come up looking similar to the next picture:

153

To locate your device, under the Missing Device section, single left click the "Find My Phone" button. The missing device menu will come up.

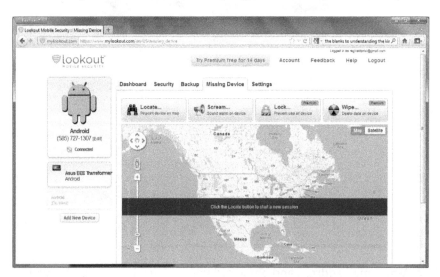

There are four things you can do remotely from this menu. You can

1. Locate your device – When you click this button, the lookout program will start tracking your device as accurate as 10 meters and send you an email that you can forward to authorities to recover your device.

2. Scream Mode (WARNING! The scream is VERY LOUD!)– If you think you have misplaced your device within your home or car, you can click this button to make the device literally "scream", so that you can find the device by hearing it.

3. Lock Mode (Premium Feature) – This feature allows you to totally lock out your device making it unusable to anyone but you.

4. Wipe Mode (Premium Feature) – This feature allows you to do a remote master reset on your device, totally wiping out all information on your device.

To start locating your device, single left click the "Locate" button and the process will start as shown in the next picture:

This window alerts you that you are about to start device location. Single left click the "Locate" button to locate your device as shown in the next picture:

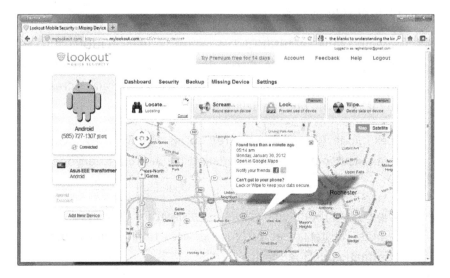

When your device is located, an email will be sent to you and the exact location (Up to 10 meters) will be displayed on the map as shown in this picture. This is how you would use lookout to locate your missing device.

But the final thing you can do for data's safety is make sure that you know where you put your Device at ALL TIMES!!!

Using a combination or all of these methods listed above will keep your data and your Device safe from would be cyber thieves and other threats.

Other Cool Things To Do With Your Android 4 Device

You Can Create And Edit Microsoft Office Documents Using A Free App Called Kingsoft Office.

Kingsoft Office is known as the most user-friendly mobile office program. Whether on a small cell phone screen or on a large tablet screen, Kingsoft Office offers the only mobile office app that comes with full-features for FREE!

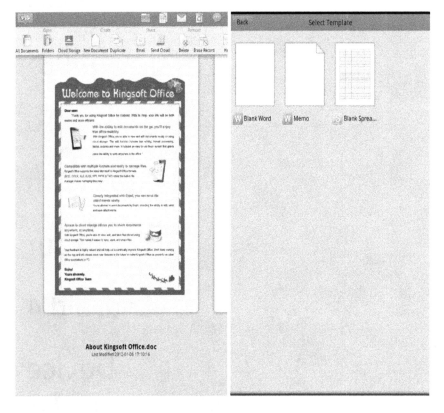

You can download and install this app from the Android Market and start creating and editing Microsoft Office Documents On Your device!

Your Android Device has the ability to print to regular printers using the popular free app EasyPrint and Google's Cloud Print Service.

First, you are going to have Google Chrome Web Browser (located at http://www.google.com/chrome) downloaded and installed on the PC or Mac computer you have printer(s) directly connected to and having the EasyPrint app installed on your Android Device from the Android Market.

Note – Before doing the following steps, you would need to have to have a Gmail or a Google account already setup. First go to http://www.gmail.com to signup for a FREE account.

Open up the Google Chrome web browser on your PC or Mac and the screen should look like the next picture:

Then move your mouse cursor to the settings menu by single left clicking your mouse on the icon which looks like a wrench, and the options menu will come up. Single left click the "Options" link.

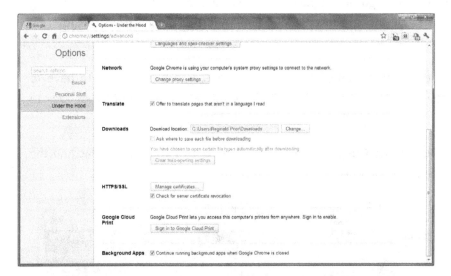

In this menu, single left click the "Under The Hood" wording. After you single clicked the "Under The Hood" option, scroll down to the "Google Cloud Print" option and single left click the "Sign In To Google Cloud Print" button. Next, sign into your Google account and the printer confirmation screen will come up as shown in the next picture:

Single click the Blue "Finish Printer Registration" button and the Thanks page will come up as shown in the next picture:

Now all of your printers that are installed on that computer are now connected to the Google Cloud Print Service and when you single left click the blue "Manage Your Printers" link, you will be taken to the Google Cloud Print main menu as shown in the next picture:

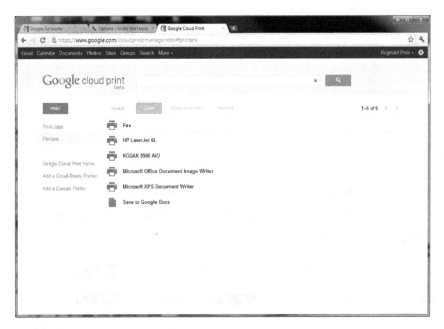

Single left click the "Printers" link on the left side of this screen and a list of all of your printers will show up here. This concludes setting up cloud printing on your computer. The next step is to connect your Android Device to Google's cloud printing service through the EasyPrint App so that you can start printing from your device.

To do this, navigate to the Android Market and search for "EasyPrint" in the search bar. (If you need detailed instructions on how to download and install apps from the Android Market, refer to page 125) After installing EasyPrint, you will see the EasyPrint Icon in the launch menu as shown in the next picture:

Single tap on it and the program will come up as shown in the next picture:

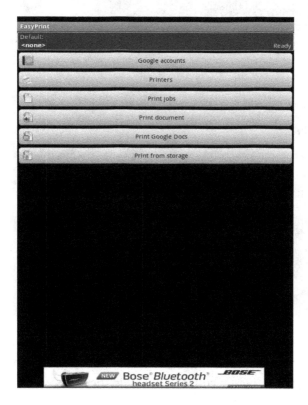

The first thing you have to do upon opening EasyPrint is to add your Google account to the program by single tapping the "Google Accounts" button. The Google Accounts menu will come up similar to the next picture:

Next, single tap the "Add" button at the bottom of this screen and a screen will come up where you would enter your username and password to your Google account as shown in the next picture:

Type in your Google Account username and password, then single tap the "Login" button to connect to Google's Cloud Print service. Single tap the back arrow key to go back to the main menu.

Next, we have to select a default printer for EasyPrint to use when printing documents or anything else from our Android device. Single tap the "Printers" button, and all of your printers that was loaded to Google's Cloud print will be listed here as shown in the next picture:

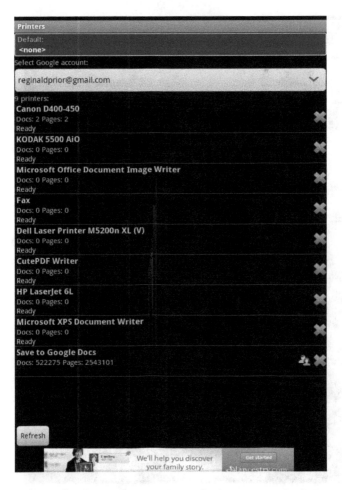

To select one of these printers as the default printer, single tap on one of them. In this example, I am going to select my Canon D400 printer. When you do that, the Default setting at the top of this menu will change from <none> to the Canon Printer. After selecting a printer from this menu, single tap the back arrow button to go back to the main menu. At this point, we are ready to select a document to print to our printer from our Android device!

To actually print a saved document on our device, single tap the "Print Document" button, and then you will be taken to the main directory on your Android device's internal memory as shown in the next picture:

Earlier I had created a document in Kingsoft Office that I wish to print. This program saves all documents in the "Documents" folder. So I single tap on that folder to open it and view the document as shown in the next picture:

To print the document, single tap the checkbox on the right side of the document to choose it, then single tap the "Print" button. The document will be sent to your printer. To go back to the previous folder, single tap the Folder icon on the top right part of the screen,

and you will go back to the previous folder.

Also you can print directly from apps and other sections within Android apps itself if it supports the share function  such as within the picture gallery section as shown in the next picture:

Note – It will take anywhere from 30 seconds to 1 minute for the document to start actually printing. That is because the document has to be transferred from your Kindle to the Google Cloud Print Service and then to your printer.

Many People Don't Know That You Can Use Your Android Device As A GPS Device!

To start using the navigation program, go to the main screen (You would get to the main screen by pressing the "Home" key on your Device. It would look like this)Single tap the launch button icon and swipe left or right to locate the navigation icon, which looks like this

 Single tap this icon, and the main navigation screen will come up similar to the next picture:

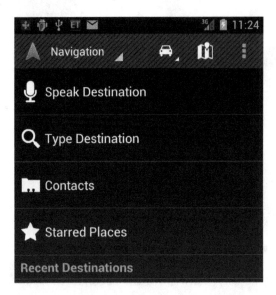

When you arrive at this screen, it is going to ask you to either type in your destination or speak it to your phone. If you single tap the "Speak Destination" option, then the speech to text feature will be enabled and you say the address and the city and state and the phone will enter what you say and start giving you directions. But in this case, I am going to single tap the "Type Destination" option, and the text keyboard will appear ready for you to type in your destination as shown in the next picture:

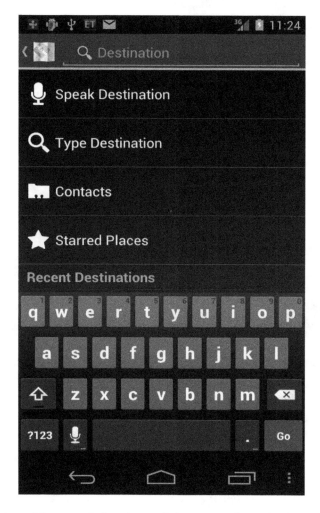

Type in the address and the city and the state, then single tap the blue "Go" key on your touch keyboard and the navigation program will start, find the GPS, and give you turn-by-turn directions as shown in the next pictures:

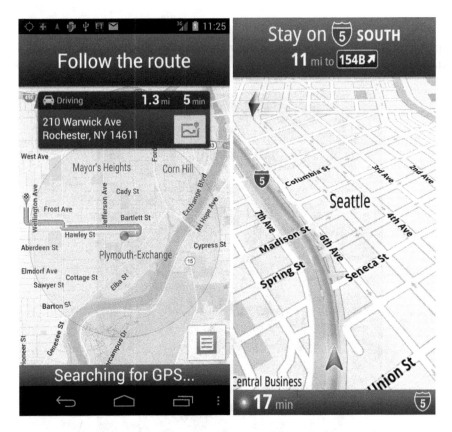

When you are done with navigation, just single tap the home key to go back to the home screen.

I hope that you have gained a lot of knowledge in learning more about your Android 4 device by reading this book. Just like in the preface, you are the most important critic and value all of your feedback about this book so that I can improve future texts. Thank you for reading and look forward to hearing from you!!

www.ingramcontent.com/pod-product-compliance
Lightning Source LLC
Chambersburg PA
CBHW071156050326
40689CB00011B/2139